You Can't Spoil an Orphan

But It Doesn't Hurt to Try

Jack vanHartesvelt

Hartland Hotels Press

You Can't Spoil an Orphan: But It Doesn't Hurt to Try

Jack vanHartesvelt

ISBN: 979-8-9988759-0-8

Published by: Hartland Hotels Press

Jack vanHartesvelt – Partner
Hartland Hotel Group
5783 Caruth Haven Ln. Unit 125
Dallas, Texas 75206
206-369-1193
www.hartlandhotelgroup.com

Jack vanHartesvelt is available to speak at your business, community, or conference event on leadership, faith, and business. Call (206) 369-1193 for more information.

About the Author

Jack vanHartesvelt's journey in the hospitality industry has been guided by a foundational belief that mission-centered living and business must coexist and are not opposites. This conviction has shaped his approach to leadership, community development, and ministry support throughout his career.

In 2013, Jack co-founded Hartland Hotel Group with his brother, Mark. The company's involvement in various US-based hotel projects reflects Jack's commitment to creating spaces that serve both guests and the broader community. Significantly, the skills, relationships, and resources developed through the hotel business became the foundation for renovating an orphanage in Mexico—demonstrating how business success can directly enable ministry opportunities that might otherwise remain unrealized.

Jack's career has been marked by transformational leadership across multiple hospitality companies. At Residence Inn, he served as Senior Development Officer during the company's expansion from 4 to 65 hotels before its acquisition by Holiday Inn. As founding President of Hawthorn Suites, he built the brand from inception before its sale to the Pritzker family. His leadership continued at Wyndham Hotel Company, where he helped grow the company from 17 to 90 hotels through its public offering, and at Westin Hotel Company, where he oversaw significant expansion across North and South America before the company's acquisition by Starwood Lodging.

As a Private Equity Fund manager and Managing Partner at Kennedy Associates Real Estate Counsel, Jack applied his development expertise to over $1.0 billion in hotel-related assets. His work contributed to the firm's remarkable growth before its sale to Bentall, experiences that deepened his understanding of stewardship and community impact through business.

Throughout his career, Jack has championed the creation of distinctive hospitality experiences, often developing properties that became brands unto themselves. Notable projects include the Liberty Hotel in Boston, The Madison Hotel in Washington DC, and the Hotel Figueroa in Los Angeles. His vision for adaptive reuse brought new life to historic structures like the W Union Square in New York City, Loews New Orleans, the Liberty Hotel in Boston (a former jail), and the W San

Diego. These lifestyle hotels required innovative food and beverage operations that served local communities, creating gathering places that extended beyond traditional hospitality.

Jack earned his Bachelor of Arts degree from Michigan State University's School of Hotel Restaurant and Institutional Management, where he was designated outstanding alumni in 1984. His commitment to integrating faith and business is reflected in his service on the Board of Directors of Seattle Pacific University's School of Business and Economics, the Center for Integrity in Business, and as Chairman of the Board of Bakke Graduate University. Through these roles and his business ventures, Jack continues to demonstrate how entrepreneurial success can be leveraged for Christian community development and transformational leadership.

Table of Contents

Chapter 1

A Neighbor's Request

While my wife, Beverly, and I were going through a period of quiet celebration, I received a call from the man who lived in the house adjoining our waterfront property on Mercer Island, Washington. The property was about 500 yards from our home, and I had spent eighteen months rezoning it to allow two homes to be built where there was presently just one. The neighbor asked that I come by at my earliest convenience so we could discuss something important. I knew our neighbor's 17-year-old son had been diagnosed with cancer and had recently undergone a bone marrow transplant.

Earlier, I had volunteered to be the bone marrow donor for his son, but the lab tests showed I was not a proper match. I thought my neighbor might want to talk about his son. I went alone to their house that evening where we met in their living room overlooking Lake Washington. Once we settled into our seats, both the husband and the wife looked distraught as he started explaining the reason for the meeting. Based on their son's last hospital visit, his doctor concluded that the bone marrow transplant had not worked, and they were now out of options. He said they could continue with the chemotherapy, which would extend his life for a short time, but it also would lower his immunity to other potential infections. Even with the chemotherapy, which they had decided to continue, his life expectancy would be somewhere between a few weeks and a few months. When he said that, his wife started to cry as if she was in great physical pain. I could feel my heart breaking but didn't know what to say.

He then said that his son would be there at home until he died and that, given his low immunity, they didn't want me to tear down the house next door until after he passed. Based on some research they had done, they believed that there could be pollens or bacteria in the walls that could be deadly to their son. I gently asked if their son could stay with his grandmother, who lives about a half mile away, for a few weeks during the demolition, and they said no, because those could end up being his final days, and they wanted him to be home with them.

"Will you agree to not tear down the house while our son is still alive?" he asked.

"I need to talk with my wife and the people who have half of the property under contract. It shouldn't take too long. I'll call you tomorrow and let you know," I replied.

When I left their house, I already knew the answer to his question. There was no way that I would risk harming their son by tearing down the house on our property. I could have told him that right away but wanted to include Beverly in the decision since she is my partner in life. I also needed to let the people who had a contract to buy half of the property know that we would not be able to close on the sale until after the house was demolished, since half of it was on the property they would be buying.

When I got home, I asked Beverly to join me on the back porch so none of our four children could overhear the discussion. I explained the family's request and the reason for it. Her reaction was the same as mine, and we agreed without any debate that we would not demolish the house on our property until after nature had taken its course with their son.

I then called the couple who had the contract to buy half the property and asked if they could meet with me sometime the following day. They agreed, and we scheduled the meeting at their house on Mercer Island. They were aware of the boy's cancer but, like me, did not think that this was going to have any effect on our transaction or the construction of their new home. I explained the new circumstances and then said that we should either delay the closing or mutually agree that the old house would have to remain standing until after the boy's death. I couldn't say with any certainty if the property sale would be in two weeks, two months, or six months.

The wife, who was a high-profile Seattle lawyer, said, "We did not sign up for this. I'm sorry that the family is having to go through this, but it's none of our business, and I don't want to get involved. If we're not going to complete the sale as stated in the contract, then we want out."

I said, "I understand your reluctance and wish there was another option that did not put the boy's final days at risk. I'll send to you a notice of termination and return your security deposit since none of this is of your doing."

The meeting didn't last very long after that because, after the painful conclusion was reached, none of us were interested in socializing. On the way home, I did some mental math and calculated what this was going to cost me every month until I could put the property back on the market. I could afford it, but it was not going to be comfortable.

I called the neighbor later that evening and told him that we would honor their request. He seemed to appreciate the decision and quick reply. This had clearly been weighing on his entire family.

Chapter 2

Previous Success and More to Come

The reason Beverly and I were celebrating was twofold.

In August 2001, I was a partner at Kennedy Associates, a large private equity firm based in Seattle, Washington. I oversaw all hotel-related investments from identification, design, construction, management oversight, and ultimately the disposition of the hotels we purchased or built. Since most of our pension fund clients were construction unions, they favored investments in to-be-built hotels so their members would have work they might not have had otherwise, as well as making money on the property for their retirement fund.

Before joining the private equity firm, I had been a minority partner in two hotel companies that went public on the New York Stock Exchange, so on the family level, I was financially comfortable and wasn't concerned about my ability to pay my family's living expenses. I lived on Mercer Island, which is an island in Lake Washington between Seattle and Bellevue, which are the two largest cities in the State of Washington.

Because of the success of our initial hotel investments, Kennedy Associates agreed to raise a new fund that would only invest in hotels in which I would be a major shareholder and oversee all its transactions. So the first celebration was that by August 2001, we had been approved by enough investors to finalize all the legal documents and begin the investing process.

And the second was the waterfront house on Mercer Island I had spent eighteen months rezoning to allow for two homes to be built on its land, the plan being to sell one of the lots and to build a home for ourselves on the second lot.

Now that the buyer of the first lot had withdrawn and the uncertainty of when we could find a replacement, this fun opportunity had become a source of concern.

Chapter 3

The World Changes

Less than a month after our waterfront project was put on hold, on the morning of September 11, 2001, we were woken by a call from Beverly's mother telling us to turn on the news. Seattle is three time zones behind New York, and we hadn't yet learned of the events that occurred earlier that morning. Like everyone, we were shocked at the news coverage and concerned about what would follow as New York City and the entire country processed the implications.

One of the hotels our company owned, the W Hotel - Union Square, was the first hotel north of the barricades in Manhattan. I tried calling our general manager, but the telephone service was jammed. I composed an email instead, telling him how I thought he should respond. When I was in charge of development at Wyndham Hotels, we had twelve hotels in the Caribbean, and every year at least one of them was hit by a hurricane. Sometimes the damage was modest, but occasionally it was devastating.

Having witnessed how our local employees responded during the storms and shortly thereafter, I thought my insights would be helpful for the W Hotel's team. During a major crisis, like a hurricane, many of our Caribbean employees wouldn't leave the hotel and return home, even when given permission to do so. They chose to stay and protect the hotel and its guests as best they could. Even after the storm had passed, those brave men and women were reluctant to return to their homes. In my email to the general manager, I told him that we should allow the employees to move into the hotel with their families if that made them feel more comfortable, that we should make the hotel a relief center for the first responders, and allow our current hotel guests to stay as long as they needed to until they could arrange for transportation home. The wisdom was well-received and our employees, our guests, the first responders, and the local residents who stumbled into the hotel covered in dust were properly cared for on that day and, for some, in the days and weeks that followed.

But the wider impact of 9/11 hit fast. Planes were grounded. People were afraid. Hotel occupancy plummeted. What I could not help with was the negative impact this had on publicly traded stocks and people's reluctance to travel on an airplane. Most people who rent hotel rooms in major US markets arrive by airplane, so if the whole country does not feel safe flying on a commercial carrier, then most hotel rooms will be empty. Fear of airline travel depressed hotel revenues all across the country, resulting in greatly reduced profits in the first few months that followed the terrorist attack. No one knew when or if the US travel industry was going to return to the healthy state it was in prior to 9/11. That uncertainty caused the value of publicly traded hotel stocks to go down, as well as our company's quarterly valuation of our hotel assets.

In the private equity business, where pension funds are the investors, the fees earned are based on the equity value of the properties. As a consequence of the 9/11 event, my partnership income was considerably reduced, as was the value of the hotel stocks that I owned. Further, the pension funds that had agreed to invest in my hotel fund all called to say that they did not think that investing in hotels at that time was a good idea.

From mid-August to mid-September in 2001, I had gone from being very financially comfortable with more very good things about to begin… to being financially insecure without a clear understanding of how it would all get back on track. Instead of dreaming about the even better days to come, I was having to consider selling our stocks in a down-market, selling our waterfront property to someone who didn't want to build anything new, and, worst case, having to sell our home.

I spent my days working with the management of our hotels on how to navigate their way through the public's fear of travel and my nights planning how my family was going to maintain its standard of living. It was all very stressful. At the center of it all was the waterfront property. We had a $1,300,000 loan on the property, with the interest rate priced for a real estate acquisition of unentitled land. This is what it was because our intent was to rezone it for two houses. At the time of acquisition, the lender knew we weren't going to be living in the house that was there at the time and that there was a lot of work ahead with the city's planning department. The monthly payments, under our current circumstances, had become painful.

Chapter 4

A Pastoral Experience

I received a call in late September from Dale Sewall, the senior pastor of Mercer Island Presbyterian Church, which is the church Beverly and I attend. He invited me to join him for lunch one day.

While everything else was going on, I was also overseeing a $6,000,000 renovation and expansion of the church, which was going very well. I thought he probably wanted an update on the status of the project, and I needed to find a way to tell him that the $100,000 donation I committed to for the renovation was now at risk.

Once we got past the pleasantries and settled into our church conversation over lunch, he asked me, "So, how are you doing?"

I gave him a quick summary of the construction status of the church, concluding that we remain on time and on budget.

He seemed pleased and then asked, "So, how are you doing?"

I figured this time he was asking about my day job, so I gave him an elevator speech on the challenges of being in the hotel business at that time.

His expression changed to one of mild concern, and then he asked once again, "So, how are you doing?"

If he was going to keep pressing with that same question, I decided that now would be a good time to tell him about the uncertainty of our $100,000 donation. I explained to him how the waterfront property was the primary cause of this and how the situation with the neighbor's son limited our options. He said they'd find a way to cover our donation amount, if need be.

Then he asked me again. "So, how are you doing?"

In a typical year, I can count the number of times I shed a tear on one hand. To be clear, that is not saying that I cry five times. It means that, on average, only five tears of sorrow come out of my eyes in a year. Well, after his last question, I shed about a two-year supply. During that weep, I explained in more detail our reaction to the news about the young man's cancer, our decision to honor the parents' request, and the financial hardship it was causing in this post-9/11 environment.

Like a good pastor, he listened with great empathy, and when I was finished, he said, "You shouldn't have to bear this alone. Let me make a couple of phone calls and see if there is someone willing to help you get through this."

To this day, I cannot decide why he kept asking the same question. It was either a God thing, my wife clued him in, or he was using his many years of pastoral experience to see deeper into my heart.

Chapter 5

An Amazing Gift

Within a couple of days, I received a call from a fellow parishioner who made his living as a litigator. He had been awarded some large settlements over his career and wanted to use some of the proceeds for a good cause. I explained to him my situation and the amount of money I thought it would take to get us through the rough patch ahead.

After a slight pause at the end of my explanation, he agreed to lend me the full amount that I requested and wished me good luck with the challenges I was facing.

It's hard to describe in a few words how much this lowered the stress in my life. I still had to navigate the effects of the 9/11 event on our hotels and hopefully find a way to convince the pension fund investors who previously agreed to invest in our hotel fund to renew their commitment. This was all definitely a challenge with an unknown final outcome, but at least my family's economic stability was restored. I was able to sleep better at night and use calm business logic to plot the strategy we took over the next few months.

I have found that all pension fund investors can be categorized into two groups. The first are pension fund advisors who think that the current economic conditions will continue for the foreseeable future, and they seek investments that make sense in that context. The second group are pension fund advisors who can see beyond the current economic conditions and can envision, with confidence, how the economic trends will change over the next few years.

In the process of making presentations to pension funds and their advisors about countercyclical investments, one of the first questions the people in the first group would ask is, "Can you send to us a report by one of the major news outlets that supports what you are proposing?"

With that one question, I knew that they could never see beyond the current economic condition and needed a third party to tell them that their perception of the economy was incorrect before they could consider approving the investment. Fortunately, the pension funds that had agreed to invest in my hotel fund before 9/11 were part of the second group because they understood countercyclical investing. They just needed to get beyond the panic of 9/11 and be reminded of our strategy, which was to "Buy low and sell high."

I thought the best way to get the investors to move past the panic and re-embrace the investment strategy was to come up with a simple and, hopefully, quotable phrase that bore the message. In early November 2001, I wrote a status report on the hotel fund, with the target audience being the pension funds and their advisors. The goal was to acknowledge that we were delaying the activation of the fund until they were comfortable that the period of economic disruption from 9/11 had passed.

In December and January, there was enough of an economic recovery and a restoration of calm with the general public that the investors agreed that we should finish up the legal documents and get them signed so we could move forward with the investments. By February 2002, the hotel fund documents were signed, and the hotels we already owned were performing almost as well as they had done prior to 9/11.

****

The young man with cancer who lived next to our waterfront property was still alive. The prognosis had not changed, but he held on longer than the doctors thought he would.

I met with a real estate broker who was active on Mercer Island to see if it would be possible to sell the property to someone who would agree to not tear down the house at least for a while. He said that it was possible, but given the house's state of disrepair, the value might be less than I paid for it. If all someone had to do was wait a short period of time before they could tear it down and build two others, then the value might have been the same or more than my purchase price. But the city's permission to build two houses on that property had expired in November 2001, and the process to renew that entitlement would take a year, without a guaranteed successful outcome.

We decided to put the property up for sale in February 2002 to get rid of the debt from the bank and the charitable loan from our fellow parishioner. By the end of March 2002, the waterfront property was sold at a loss but with the contractual agreement that the new owner would not tear down the house until after the young man living next door had passed away. In mid-April of 2002, that sad day finally came.

Incurring the loss in property value was painful. But with the expensive monthly payments gone, having the economy return to stabilization, and getting my hotel fund agreements fully executed seemed like a blessing. The outcome would have been very different if my fellow parishioner had not come forth when he did and with exactly what I needed. What he gave was very easy for him to provide, but it was something that I could not do on my own.

I wanted to find a way to pay him back for rescuing us in our time of need, but neither he nor his family needed anything that I could provide. After a few restless nights trying to envision something I could do for him that he would value, I concluded that maybe I should consider helping someone else who needs something I can provide that they cannot do for themselves. My simple explanation for this strategy was to "Pay it forward."

Chapter 6

Who Steals from Orphans?

One of the hotels that we were investing in was the W Hotel in downtown San Diego. In the spring of 2002, the hotel was under construction with a projected opening date of December 12, 2002. Since it was a hotel and one of our investment funds was the majority owner, I had overseen the acquisition of the land and the property's design and was now monitoring the construction process. We had a good general contractor, Webcor, with qualified union subcontractors, so everything was proceeding on schedule and on budget.

As is almost always the case with a major construction project, situations arise that we refer to as "unforeseen conditions" that need to be addressed quickly. These include contaminated soil, architectural plans that are in conflict with some of the engineering documents, and occasionally a slightly different design idea is proposed and accepted that requires modifying some aspects of the building. When one or more of these situations arise, it's important for the owner to make quick decisions to minimize the cost increase and potential delay in the property's opening. What this required from me was that I be at the construction site for at least one week every month.

Meanwhile, in April 2002, our church on Mercer Island organized a group of its high school members to go on a trip to Tijuana, Mexico, to build several small houses in one of its poverty-stricken suburbs, and then, once completed, they'd give them to local homeless families. Several churches in the Seattle area had been doing this every spring for the previous seven years and by 2001 had built and given away nearly 1,000 houses to families in need.

The students and the church leaders would stay in the Casa Hogar de Los Ninos orphanage, which translates to "Home of the Children." The orphanage was located near the community where the church would be building the little houses. The orphanage was founded by Tony Ralphs, a California resident, in 1988. His inspiration to start the orphanage had been a suggestion from Mother Teresa while he was on a mission trip in India a few years before. Tony's family started the Ralphs grocery store chain, and he had dedicated his life to charitable causes.

My daughter, Blaire, who was 18 years old in 2002, had been one of the workers on those mission trips in two prior years, and she had volunteered to participate again on the 2002 project. As in the previous two trips, she asked me to join her and build a home for a family in need. I had always declined to go because building a small house in a troubled neighborhood didn't seem like a good use of my talent. I had planned and overseen the development of over 100 hotels by then, and if I was going to be involved, it seemed like it should be with something more challenging.

This time when she asked me to join her, I also said no, but these rejections were starting to make me feel like a bad father. So, I tried explaining to her that I would be willing to help out, but I needed the work to be more challenging. I thought giving her an example might help make the point, so I suggested that helping the orphans might be a better use of my skills. Perhaps what we could do is buy them a lot of computers and have a missionary with technology skills teach them computer programming. The orphans would enjoy having computers as a source of entertainment, and they would learn an important skill that could help them find a job when they got older. Her reaction was not what I expected.

She said, "You should not give them computers. They live in a dangerous neighborhood, and people are always stealing from them. Having a lot of computers would create a serious safety problem."

Her comment not only made the computer idea seem like a mistake, it also caused me to be concerned about the orphans' safety. Who steals from orphans? I tried to shake it off, but her words kept haunting my thoughts. It was the last thing I thought of before going to sleep and the first thought I had when I got up in the morning.

After about two weeks of dealing with this nightmare, I decided that I had to go to the orphanage and convince Tony Ralphs and the on-site manager to let me build a security fence around the orphanage to keep the orphans safe.

Chapter 7

A Meeting of Minds

My next trip to San Diego, which is right across the border from Tijuana, was at the end of April 2002. Once there, I scheduled a private meeting with Webcor's project manager on our hotel, Ken Summers. I explained to him the unsafe conditions at the orphanage and that I wanted to build a security fence around it. And if he was willing, I needed his help getting the materials and recruiting the labor. If we had enough volunteers with the right skills, I thought we should be able to build the fence in one weekend.

I was pleased that he wanted to help. He also thought this would be something that the owner of the construction company, Ross Edwards Sr., and the owner's son, Ross Edwards Jr., might like to help with because they sponsor a charity construction event every year. The volunteer effort is called Christmas in April, and they organize a team of volunteers to fix up a local building that's used to serve the community.

I thought that this could be very helpful and encouraged Ken to make the call. To my surprise, he dialed Ross Jr.'s phone number while I was standing there, and once he answered, Ken described what I was proposing and asked if this was something he would like to help with. I could only hear one side of the conversation, but they seemed to be having an energetic exchange. Once the call was over, Ken said that they definitely wanted to help and that Ross would like to go with me during my next visit to the orphanage.

Now that I had a capable construction company willing to coordinate the work, I had to make certain the orphanage's owner agreed that this was needed and that he would support the effort. I called Tony Ralphs, and he said that it sounded like a very good idea and that he'd like to be at the orphanage during our visit to show us around and express his appreciation. I asked him when his next scheduled trip was to Tijuana.

"In three days," he said.

"Let me see if I can get the team together and meet you there."

In light of everyone's busy schedule, I was amazed that all the invitees were able to visit the orphanage three days later.

That night, as I was feeling encouraged by the warm reception that my proposed security fence was having, I thought about my fellow parishioner who helped me in a way that I could not help myself at the time. Maybe this was going to be the way I could pay it forward. Organizing a fence-building project fit my skill set. It felt like it was truly needed, and it was something the orphanage's sponsor and caregivers had not been able to do for themselves.

Three days later, Ken Summers, Ross Edwards Jr., Scott Murfey (a construction consultant), and I crossed the US/Mexican border and headed toward the Casa Hogar de Los Ninos orphanage.

Chapter 8

You Can't Spoil an Orphan

In the years leading up to 2002, Tijuana was rated as one of the most dangerous cities in the world, and 2002 was no exception. In several of those years, it was actually number one on the list. The orphanage was about ten miles south and west of the border crossing in a community known to be one of the most dangerous in Tijuana. Sewage was processed in septic tanks for many of the houses, and very few of the buildings were officially connected to the city's electrical network.

On the drive to the orphanage, we saw that several homeowners had attached a metal clothes hanger to a wire and tossed the hanger over one of the city's electrical cables. They then attached the other end of the wire to a junction box inside their house. This was not the safest way to get electrical power into their home, but it eliminated the cost until someone from the city's utility department made them remove the hanger.

The roads were in poor condition, with many potholes along the way. It took about forty-five minutes to go the ten miles from the border to the orphanage. The advice we were given before the visit was to not go anywhere alone and to stay inside when the sun went down. Completing that short trip without incident was a relief.

Meeting Tony Ralphs was a pleasure, as was hearing about his time in India with Mother Teresa and how he started the orphanage in Tijuana. After the initial greeting and storytelling, we got our first tour of the Casa Hogar de Los Ninos compound. The property started out as a small Catholic church, with the chapel and offices still there but no longer being used. There was a small kitchen and dining area in the main dormitory building with the restrooms in the basement.

The orphanage manager, Rosa Camacho, led us down to the basement to see the restrooms. Once there, she pointed to one of the toilet stalls and said that it was the only one that was working.

"How many orphans live here?" I asked her.

She said, "We have fifty-five children."

"You have fifty-five children and only one working toilet?"

"Yes."

"Is this something that the city could come and fix?"

"We have our own septic tank for the bathrooms, so the city can't help with the problem."

Later, we went up to the second floor to inspect the bedrooms. All the rooms were shared, with most having bunk beds, allowing four to six children to be assigned to each room. As we were finishing up the tour, Rosa pointed to a good-sized section of the second floor that was unusable because it had to be accessed from the outside. The stairs that were there originally had to be torn down due to advanced disrepair.

That evening we had dinner with the children in the dining room. Having negotiated hundreds of legal agreements over the previous fifteen years, I learned how to read people based on their facial expressions and body language. There were a lot of conversations underway between the children, with most of them smiling and appearing to be engaged. Even though they were living in a dilapidated dormitory, they seemed to be comfortable. At least they had a bed to sleep in, food to eat, and they were living with a group of children who were all going through the same life journey.

After dinner was over, but while the kids were still in the dining room, Ross and I walked across the street to a small convenience store to see if they had any sweet treats for sale. All they had were ice cream bars, and there weren't very many. Ross decided to buy every one they had, hoping it would be enough for all the children to get at least one. We put them in a small box and walked back over to the orphanage's dining room to give them away. The kids were very excited about having a dessert since they didn't get one very often. Rosa had them line up and go one at a time past Ross so he could hand them an ice cream bar. This was a fun way to end our tour. As I stood a few feet back from Ross watching the procession, I saw that a few of the older children were cutting back into the line after they had their ice cream bar. Several of them ended up getting two ice cream bars, and one of them even got three before we ran out!

As we drove home later that evening, I asked Ross if he had seen that some of the kids had gone through the line more than once.

He said, "Yeah. I saw that."

"I didn't want to say anything."

After a slight pause, Ross said, "You can't spoil an orphan."

Based on having witnessed their difficult living conditions and knowing that this was the only family that most of them had ever known, I found his comment about spoiling an orphan to be painful. It didn't take very long for my eyes to start tearing up. Apparently, all four of us in the car were having the same reaction because no one talked for several minutes after that.

As we were coming up to the border crossing, I asked the other guys if they were still on board with building the security fence.

Scott Murfey said, "It feels like a good project, but only having one working toilet for fifty-five orphans is a problem. I think we should get a plumber to come down and see if they can get the bathrooms working right while we're doing the security fence."

"I like that idea," I said. "Do you know a plumbing company that might be interested?"

"I think the one that's working on the hotel would be a good place to start."

The next day, Ken and Scott met with the plumbing subcontractor's owner and asked him if he'd be willing to fix the toilets at the orphanage. He said he might consider it but would need to go there first and assess the problem. Fortunately, I was able to stay an extra day in San Diego and joined them on the inspection. After several hours of investigation, the plumber determined that either the septic tank was nearly full or the pipes were clogged. He also noted that the showers were not working properly and that, based on fifty-five orphans living there, they needed to add at least one new bathroom.

When he finished outlining the scope of the work, I asked, "Is this something that you can get done in one weekend?"

A little smile came to his face, and he said, "I could probably do it in two days, but I would need several months to plan out the details and about thirty plumbers on the workdays."

To this, I replied, "We'll probably schedule the work weekend late in the fourth quarter, after the hotel's opening. That would give you plenty of time for planning. Can you recruit thirty volunteer plumbers?"

"I'll check around and let you know. By the way, did you notice the bars on the windows? That creates a safety hazard. Tijuana might not have a building code that prevents bars from being on the windows meant for escape, but you should make sure that the possibility of a fire is minimized. The one potential area of risk that I saw was the electrical wiring. There were several exposed wires and at least one junction box that did not have the right capacity. If you're going to fix up this orphanage, you should do what you can to make sure it doesn't burn down."

The old adage of "Ignorance is bliss" has some application here. The scope of work had grown from building a security fence to now include fixing the plumbing and maybe having to rewire the orphanage's entire electrical system. Now that I knew of these problems, I couldn't pretend that they didn't exist.

***

On my next visit to San Diego, I scheduled a trip to Tijuana with an electrician who Ken Summers had asked to assess the situation and would maybe agree to do the work.

After about a three-hour examination by the electrical contractor and his team, they concluded that several sections of the orphanage needed to be rewired and that all the equipment in the electrical room should be replaced. I asked the company's owner, who was leading the on-site investigation, if this work could be completed in two days.

In response, he said, "Maybe… if I had forty electricians and every piece of equipment we needed was here when we arrived."

I said, "The best way to be sure that you have all the materials and equipment you need is to bring it with you when you come. Do you think that forty of your employees will volunteer for the weekend of work?"

"I don't have forty employees, and of the eighteen I do have, I can't guarantee that all will commit to the project. I can tell you, though, that I would personally commit to doing this and would have a plan completed well before the actual workdays. So, do you think you can recruit another thirty electricians to work with us?"

"Thank you for agreeing to take the lead on this. Helping to keep these children safe is what we're trying to do with this repair work, and your part of this is essential. Let's assume for now that we'll be able to recruit the extra electricians. We've got about six months to find them, and we will keep you updated on the number who have agreed to come."

The electrical company's owner nodded his head in agreement and then said, "Did you know that the mechanical equipment is broken, and it can't generate any heat? It's only cold down here once in a while in the winter months, but on those days it would be very uncomfortable in a building with no heat."

I told him that we'd have someone check it out. Then I glanced over at Ken. He didn't have to say anything. I knew what he was thinking, which was that this project was starting to become quite large for a weekend charity event.

When we got back to San Diego, I met with the renovation team to discuss the expanding scope of work and make sure they were still willing to take it on. They said they agreed that the physical problems with the orphanage needed to be fixed and that they remained committed to seeing it through to the finish. It was going to take some extra time to plan because some of what was being discussed would take several weeks or even a couple of months to complete at a normal commercial construction job. Once you factor in that all this work was going to take place at the same time, a more realistic time frame to do everything would have been 3–4 months because fewer workers are typically assigned to a task by each of the subcontractors, and the work is usually phased so two or more trades are not working in the same part of the building on the same day.

I was not familiar with the operational logistics of doing a project of this scale in a compressed period of time. I recall hearing about how the early US settlers would get together on a weekend for a barn raising, where a large group of people would build a barn for one of their neighbors in 1–2 days. While I'm sure it was an impressive accomplishment, no barns of that era had electrical wiring, fully functional bathrooms, heating and air-conditioning, a kitchen, telephone cabling, framed glass windows, or floors made of wood, tile, or carpet!

The construction team explained to me that every aspect of this project had to be planned in detail, with all the materials and tools needed to complete the project being on-site when the workers arrive. Further, we had to recruit enough skilled workers in each of the disciplines to complete the full scope of work. There were ways to make the process more efficient, but even with a perfect execution, a certain number of man-hours would be required to complete each project.

It seemed like one of the ways to make sure we had enough skilled tradesmen on the workdays was to also recruit unskilled workers whose only qualification was to have a strong back and a willing heart. Much of the work would involve hauling materials from a truck to where they were needed on the jobsite, cleaning up throughout the process, fetching tools, or communicating nontechnical information like "We need three more plumbers in the basement." Anytime we could get an unskilled volunteer to do this part of the work, it would allow the skilled tradesmen to spend more of their time on the parts that required their specialized skill set. Based on this assumption, it seemed like I was going to have to recruit some volunteers from outside the construction trades.

Chapter 9

Getting the Workers

I returned to Mercer Island feeling a bit overwhelmed. My two-day security fence project had become a lot more complicated. This was going to require a lot more workers, time to plan it all out, and we needed to get companies with the materials to donate them, or this new scope of work was going to be very expensive.

I called Dale Sewall, our church pastor, and asked him if I could have a few minutes during the next Sunday's worship services to explain the project to the congregation and ask for volunteers to help on the work weekend. He said that this would be fine and suggested that I meet with a couple of the church leaders who oversee the Tijuana home-building project that the church sponsors. Dale thought getting them involved might help, given that they had construction skills and were familiar with the orphanage. This sounded like a good idea, and I agreed to call one of the leaders who owned a construction company and whom I had known for over ten years. His name was Eric Stelter and I called him later that day, and we scheduled a time to meet on the Saturday before the worship services, when I would be introducing the construction project to the congregation.

We got together in one of the meeting rooms at the church. The renovation and expansion of the church that I was overseeing on behalf of the congregation was nearly complete, with only a few finishing touches remaining. As we neared completion, I was monitoring the budget very closely. As is typical with any construction project, some areas cost a little more than planned and others cost a little less. There were a couple of items that we thought would be helpful to make a part of the renovation that were not in the original plan. My plan was to use the net savings when the renovation was completed to pay for these wish-list items. As the completion date got closer, my wish-list savings had gone down to $6,750. That was not as much as I had hoped for, but at least we were not over budget on our original $6,000,000 scope of work.

One of the last items to be completed was fixing an error in a decoration item we planned for an enclosed courtyard in the middle of the church building. All the surfaces in the courtyard were made of hard materials, like the tile floor, glass and metal walls, and the glass ceiling, which was in the shape of a pyramid. The decorative item was twelve clouds, all made of soft, white-colored fabric that was supposed to have sound-insulating material sewn inside. The clouds were attached to wires and hung from the ceiling, with their primary purpose being to deaden the background noise when the room was full of people. Without the insulation, the hard surfaces and the pyramid-shaped roof amplified the noise when the room was crowded. Unfortunately, the designer neglected to include the insulating material in the specifications, so the clouds had to be returned to the fabricator so it could make the modification.

Our project manager called me before my Saturday meeting and said, "I got the cost estimate from the manufacturer on what it will take to fix the clouds."

"Let me guess what the cost increase is going to be," I said.

"Really? Okay, give it a shot."

"My guess is $6,750."

He sounded surprised when he said, "That's exactly what they quoted. How in the heck did you come up with that number?"

"I guessed that's what it would be since that's the exact amount of money we have left in the wish-list fund.

41

I guess the bad news is that we won't be able to do anything on that list, but the good news is that we will have completed the entire renovation and expansion of the church for the exact amount we said it would be. That doesn't happen very often."

Based on the church renovation update, I was feeling good when I arrived for the meeting with Eric Stelter. He started off by saying that, in his opinion, the orphanage was in need of a lot of repairs and was pleased to learn that I was heading up the effort to fix some of the problems. I gave him a brief summary of the areas we would be addressing and asked if this was something that he could help with.

In response, Eric said, "I would look forward to working with you on the orphanage, but there are a lot more areas that need to be included in the project." He then pulled out a report he had prepared that had a long list of building parts and equipment that were either broken or were in such poor condition that they needed to be addressed to make the orphanage safer, more comfortable, and easier for the staff to operate. The items on his list that were not already on mine would approximately double the size of the project. I studied his list of deficiencies, hoping to find ones that could be eliminated, but there weren't very many. It would have been hard to say that the leaky roof was not a problem or that the broken floor tiles didn't need to be replaced.

I told him that I would talk to our general contractor in San Diego about the items on his list to see if they knew of any tradesmen who would agree to fix those areas. I also encouraged him to take the lead on some of the items on his list, recruit the volunteers, and get the materials. He said he would try, but Tijuana is about 1,300 miles from Seattle, Washington, which would greatly complicate the planning and quick execution of the items on his list. I wanted him to give it some thought, but privately I was confident that all the major items on his list were going to have to be part of the San Diego team's responsibility.

Our church had three services every Sunday. I was allowed to speak for about three minutes at each service before the start of the pastor's sermon. The congregation was aware of Casa Hogar de Los Ninos because that's where its high school students stayed when they volunteered to build the small houses that were given away every year. During my short talk, I explained that we would be repairing and expanding the orphanage so that it would be safer for the children and, once completed, it would be able to serve about twenty more children in need.

At the end of my presentation, I told them that I would be at a table in the foyer after the service and looked forward to signing up volunteers willing to go to Tijuana on the workdays to help with the construction. My hope was to get about 35–40 volunteers to agree to come. My expectation was tempered by the fact that each volunteer would have to pay for their flight to San Diego and back and up to four nights in a hotel. So, if fewer than 35–40 people agreed to come, it would be understandable.

To my amazement, over fifty people agreed that Sunday to go to the orphanage on the work weekend. Between that Sunday in late May 2002 and December 14, 2002 (the start of the work weekend), twenty-five more parishioners volunteered to go to Tijuana in person, and about fifty others helped with a charitable effort that will be explained later.

Chapter 10

The Ever-Expanding Scope

What started out as a project that 5–6 welders and I could comfortably do in two days had evolved into a complete renovation and expansion of the orphanage, requiring several hundred workers and three semitrucks full of materials. To complete this scope of work, following traditional construction methods would normally take about six months and, in 2002 US dollars, about $2 million.

As a further complication, the highly qualified leadership team from Webcor was also building a 265-room hotel for our pension fund clients, with a projected completion date one week before the work weekend at the orphanage. Recruiting enough qualified volunteers, getting all the materials donated, and planning it to the level of detail to complete a six-month construction job in two days was going to require a lot of overtime—and prayer.

What I had seen up to this point was that by simply explaining what we were planning and why, people agreed to help. I didn't have to use any salesmanship tactics. All I had to do was explain it and ask them once if they'd like to help. I could see a little adrenaline rush occurring in the ones that said "Yes," with several of them calling a day or two later wanting to confirm their commitment or that they had bought their plane ticket.

I decided early on that I would never ask anyone twice to volunteer. It was as if the ones who said "Yes" had committed long before we talked—as a matter of faith—to do something they believed that God wanted them to do. They just didn't know what it was going to be at the time. Once they heard about helping the orphans, something inside their minds said, "THAT ONE." Also, having a large group of workers who were excited to be helping seemed like the right profile for building something quickly.

A former assistant pastor at the Mercer Island Presbyterian Church had been recruited as senior pastor of a church in Southern California. While he was at the Mercer Island church, he had been actively involved in the home-building projects in Tijuana. Once he relocated to California, he sent a few high school students every year from his new church to join the Mercer Island team in building the homes. A few weeks after my Sunday presentation on the orphanage project, I received word that our former assistant pastor was willing to recruit volunteers from his new church to help on the workdays. I started to have confidence that we were going to have enough unskilled workers volunteer by mid-June 2002. The recruiting focus now needed to be on skilled workers.

On my next trip to San Diego, I visited the orphanage with Ken, Scott Murfey and a couple of our senior construction managers. The goal was to make sure that we had a clear understanding of all the details so we could recruit the right number of workers in each of the building trades. Our day was spent going through every part of the orphanage and taking detailed notes on what the man-hours would be to fix the problems and to calculate the type and amount of building materials we were going to need.

During our lunch break, the senior superintendent on the hotel project asked Rosa where the building materials were stored that the high school students used to build the homes. She said that the materials usually arrived a few days or weeks before the high school kids arrived, and they were stacked up in the backyard, close to the septic tank.

The superintendent looked concerned when she said that and replied, "I think we should build a storage shed to keep the materials from being stolen."

I said, "Every time the students come down, they build 8–10 houses. That's a lot of concrete, lumber, windows, and doors. It would have to be a pretty big storage shed." I was also thinking that this would take another five carpenters and about 1,000 pounds of wood to build.

Before the superintendent could respond, Rosa said, "We worry every time those materials are delivered that someone is going to steal them, and those families who were praying for a place to live will have to remain homeless."

Since the superintendent was going to have to take responsibility for getting the supply shed built, I decided to remain silent and let him decide whether to expand the scope.

Not to my surprise, he asked Rosa, "Can you show me the best place to build the storage shed?"

When Rosa and the superintendent walked outside to inspect her recommended area, a visitor entered the dining area. He glanced around the room for a moment and then came to where we were seated and introduced himself. He said that his church in Eastern Washington State had been working with the orphanage for the last ten years. Their main area of focus was buying Christmas presents for the orphans every year. It seemed like a worthwhile contribution in the beginning, but after ten years, many of the original volunteers had backed away, and he was finding it difficult to find enough donors for all the children. In the last couple of years, this resulted in some children not getting any presents on Christmas Day. He said that he was pleased to learn that we were going to be doing a lot of repair work on the buildings and would appreciate our agreeing to being the orphans' Santa Claus this year.

Before I had a chance to answer, he handed me several pages that listed the names of all the orphans and what they had requested this year as Christmas presents. I expected to see the kinds of things that my children would have put on their Christmas list when they were of similar age, but the items were very different. I read as many on the lists as I could before my eyes teared up and it became a blur. Almost none of the lists had more than four items, and they were all basic necessities like a pair of shoes, blue jeans, or a new pen and some lined paper for school homework. The closest thing I saw to being a toy was a request for a teddy bear. All I could think of was, "You can't spoil an orphan."

I told the man who made the Christmas present request that I would have to see if one of my fellow parishioners would take the lead on this assignment. I promised to call him with the answer within a couple of days.

I was not sure how many volunteers would be required to buy, wrap, and ship Christmas presents for fifty-five orphans. It was probably going to be more than ten but less than fifty-five, and there would need to be an organizer. As I considered who I should call to volunteer for the lead role in this effort, only one stood out: Marilee Ahalt. Her husband was a co-worker of mine. We lived on the same island and attended the same church. She was very organized and was a frequent planner of social events. I decided to give her a call when I got back to the US to see if she was willing to take this on or knew someone else I should call.

As we drove from Tijuana back to the hotel jobsite in downtown San Diego, I asked Scott Murfey if he believed we would have enough skilled tradesmen to complete this ever-expanding scope of work in two days. He was encouraged by the response he'd seen thus far, but it would be better to have a few more than we needed as opposed to a few less. To help ensure we have enough workers, he recommended that I speak directly to the people working on the hotel project and ask them to come. He also thought that it would be worth my going to one of the citywide trade union meetings once we got closer to the work weekend and explain the project. We only needed them for two days, and this had a very compelling emotional appeal.

During a lull in the conversation, Ken said that he had called the owner of a major lumber company in Southern California. They had several storage facilities in the area, and Webcor was one of their larger customers. Ken had asked the lumber company owner if he would donate the materials we needed, store them in the San Diego area, and then deliver them to the orphanage just before the work weekend. The company owner said that he would be willing to do that and also allow us to store other materials and equipment there that we had to source from other suppliers.

"That's great," I said. "How much of what we need does he have in stock?"

"Most of it in terms of volume, but there are a lot of smaller items we need that he doesn't carry," Ken said. "It's going to take some time to track everything down, and there will be some items that we'll have to buy. That's the nature of these types of projects. In summary, it's like 'free, free, free, free, 100 percent retail, free, free, free, and 100 percent retail.' The problem is that not every supplier is going to donate what we need, but we still have to have every piece or part to complete the work."

"How much do you think this is going to cost?"

"I'm not sure, but I want you to know that Webcor has agreed to contribute $30,000 to cover the gaps in material donations. We're good for now, but you should plan on coming up with a similar amount in case there are any surprises."

Chapter 11

Mixing Business with Charity

I had never experienced anything like this before. All I had done was say I wanted to build a security fence around an orphanage, and within a couple of months the scope had expanded to a full renovation of the entire facility, with people volunteering to do all the work, donate the materials, and contribute money to the project. Something was breathing life into this initiative, and it wasn't me or any of the other team leaders. When people said what they were willing to do and why, it always sounded personal. One of my friends suggested that I give the project a name that we could use to promote the project, like former President Carter did with Habitat for Humanity. That might have been a good suggestion, but what I was seeing was everyone carving their own name into the project. To them, this was

THEIR project, and I didn't want to change that perception.

It was now time to ask Marilee Ahalt if she would assume responsibility for getting the children's Christmas presents purchased, wrapped, and shipped to the hotel jobsite in San Diego. I called and explained what was needed, with the expectation that she would say yes. She did not disappoint me. I delivered to her house the list with the orphans' names and what each of them was hoping to get for Christmas that year. It took her a couple of days to recruit the volunteer Santas. I thought we'd get the presents close to Christmas Day, which was about five months from when Marilee took on the task, but about two weeks later several large boxes full of wrapped Christmas presents arrived at the San Diego hotel's jobsite. The presents were all organized by the child's name, and all fifty-five orphans were going to get the gifts they requested.

I was sharing this success story over dinner one evening, and my daughter Blaire had an interesting suggestion. She said, "With all those orphans living in the same building, I think it might be hard for them to feel like any part of it is just for them. The logical place to try and personalize is their bed. I'd be willing to sew the name of each orphan into a pillowcase and make that one of the Christmas presents they get this year."

"Do you know how to sew a name onto a pillowcase? It seems like that would take some time to learn," I said.

"I belong to a sewing club, and we learned a couple of weeks ago how to create a design with a sewing machine using different colored threads. I could ask the other club members if they'd like to help. It shouldn't take too long if they all agree."

This sounded like a great idea, and I told her to "Go for it."

By the end of the summer, the hotel construction seemed to be on schedule, and the planning for the orphanage renovation was on track. Most of the materials we needed had been shipped to the warehouse. Every few weeks someone on the leadership team would identify a new piece or part that was not yet on the list. They would make a few calls to suppliers and try to get them donated. If that didn't work, they would buy it and put it in the warehouse.

The number of committed volunteers from the skilled trades was fewer than we needed to get everything done in two days. Ken said more would agree to come when we got closer to the work weekend. In his opinion, most of the workers who would go were focused right now on completing the hotel. It's always stressful in the last few months before you open due to unexpected problems identified by city inspectors or some aspect of the hotel's complicated network of mechanical, electrical, plumbing, technology, elevators, or fire/life safety systems not performing properly. The fact that the furniture, fixtures, and equipment were being installed while these last-minute construction issues were being addressed added to the stress. Also, the hotel's operating staff was now on-site for training, which was a further distraction.

Ken reminded me that the hotel's target completion date was only seven days before the work weekend at the orphanage. As the number of construction workers at the hotel goes down during the final stages, more of them would feel comfortable committing to the busy weekend in Tijuana.

His explanation of the skilled labor count made sense. At least it lowered my own stress, caused by opening a major hotel in a large city within one week of also executing a $2 million construction project in two days in the most dangerous city in the world. Considering the complications of both projects, I found it difficult to sleep peacefully through the night. Whenever there was a brief period of time when I wasn't focused on a specific problem that had to be addressed on the hotel project, my concern about having overlooked a detail of the orphanage renovation caused me to envision the workdays and try to identify a gap in the plan. It was during one of those contemplations that I thought we should have a couple of cooks on-site with enough food for six meals over the weekend. Having professionals do the cooking and serving seemed like the right approach since there would be 200–300 workers, so the number of required meals would be between 1,200 and 1,800 over a two-day period.

I had a meeting scheduled with a senior executive of the Hotel Employees and Restaurant Employees Union (HERE) at the end of August 2002 in Los Angeles. The union would certainly know a lot of qualified cooks and servers in San Diego, and having the request for volunteers coming from someone at the national level should increase my chances of getting a positive response. The purpose of the meeting in Los Angeles was to discuss HERE's potential investment in our hotel fund. These were very different topics, but I was confident they would allow me some time to also explain the orphanage renovation and our need for a few cooks and servers. In addition to the senior HERE executive, the meeting was attended by one of the union's California-based investment advisors.

The discussion on the hotel fund went well, and they said that they would consider recommending it to several of the "locals," which is the term they use for the HERE-affiliated unions that operate in major cities around the country. Each local has its own president, who is elected by its members who are employed in that community. The pension fund investment decisions are then made by the local's senior management and their financial consultants.

When the conversation transitioned to the orphanage project, I noticed a change in their body language. It went from thoughtful and professional to one of being highly focused with a hint of adrenaline. The investment advisor was the first to respond after my explanation of the project and request for a couple of cooks who were experienced in quantity food production. He said he didn't have any culinary skills, but he was an artist who created large statues and art objects using a welding torch instead of a paintbrush.

Then he said, "If you're going to build a security fence around the orphanage, you're going to need welders. I can help you with that. When I was in high school and college, my summer jobs were as a welder on construction sites, which is where I learned the trade."

"That would be great," I said. "We need more volunteers in that area. Part of the perimeter is the exterior wall of the orphanage; part of it is a gate, there are a couple of concrete sections, and about half of it is wide open. Having someone with artistic skills who can figure out the best way to fit all the parts together would be a blessing."

The senior executive from the hotel union said, "I will call the president of the San Diego local and ask him to recruit some qualified high-volume chefs for that weekend. It shouldn't be a problem."

I told them both that I was grateful for their help with this and was sure the project would be more successful because of their efforts.

Chapter 12

A Misunderstanding and Faith

One of the lessons I learned working with the hotel unions was that they were not very good at their internal communications. Of all the misquotes I witnessed over the years, none were as bad as what was communicated to the president of the San Diego hotel union by the senior executive who was at the meeting.

Four days after my meeting with the senior executive, I received a call from the president of the San Diego HERE local. "I understand that you are working with some orphans in Tijuana and need some help getting them fed," he said. "Well, I have some good news. I talked to the head of the San Diego Convention Center, and he agreed to donate two tons of food. I also talked to the general manager of the Sheraton Hotel by the marina, and he agreed to donate three tons of food and also store the food at his hotel before it's delivered. It took me a few days to reach the owners of several of the larger restaurants in town, but collectively they agreed to donate another ton of food. So, we'll be able to deliver six tons of food for the orphans. But here is the big one. I talked to the San Diego Food Bank about the starving children, and they agreed to provide 100 percent of their food requirements for the foreseeable future. They just need someone from the orphanage to come across the border to pick it up whenever they need to restock."

I was a bit overwhelmed hearing this, and I had to take a few deep breaths before I could speak. Finally, I said, "Thank you very much. This is much appreciated. By the way, do you think you could send a couple of cooks to the orphanage on December 14 and 15 to prepare meals for the workers who will be doing the renovation? I'll have all the food supplies there that they'll need."

"No problem," he said. "I'll probably come myself. I was a banquet chef before I became president of the hotel union."

We exchanged a few pleasantries after that and then ended the call.

I sat in my office, looking out the window, and all I could think of was, "What the heck just happened?" All

I asked for was two cooks for two days, and I ended up with two cooks, six tons of food, and a commitment from the San Diego Food Bank to keep feeding the children for as long as they want. This was going to require that we build a storage room to keep the donated food, which would take another 3–4 volunteers and more materials, but it seemed like a small price to pay.

I called one of our hotels and asked them how long it would take for fifty-five children to eat six tons of food. They said they would run the numbers and call me back. About a day later, the hotel's general manager called to say that with the right mix of ingredients, six tons of food would feed fifty-five children for approximately five months.

How does this keep happening? The only conclusion I could come up with is that God wanted it to happen. All I was doing was telling people about the project as it was envisioned at that point in time. And then, without any encouragement from me, people were expanding the scope, based on some personal inspiration. Where those ideas were coming from was a mystery. Clearly, helping orphans is a universal motivator, but the scale and speed at which this project was expanding seemed to be more than just human inspiration.

Faith has been a part of my life since childhood, and I have tried to bring it to all parts of my life. I have enjoyed good outcomes in most of my business ventures when I have taken a faith-based approach. One of my personal rules is to never preach my faith in a business setting. That's contrary to biblical teachings, but it seemed to me that having my behavior and decisions be guided by strict rules of ethics was a more convincing way to show who you are than talking about your faith in a business setting. Tony Ralphs told me about a conversation he had with Mother Teresa that seemed to summarize my approach to faith at work. He said he asked her how she preaches the gospel to the people who came to her for help. Tony said she told him that she does not preach. She just does the good work and waits for them to ask her why she committed her life to helping others. Once they ask, she tells them of her faith.

I found that story to be a positive reinforcement of my own approach. In my business life, I work with people of all faiths and some with no faith. In that context, it seems more genuine to show people who you are and let them decide if you're a person of faith, based upon what they see every day.

As noted above, the Bible says Christians should profess their faith and not wait to be asked why they do what they do. The description of my approach to faith in a business setting is, therefore, intended to be an explanation and not a recommendation.

Chapter 13

Unexpected Medical Care Gift

Putting a couple of hundred people together in a relatively small space with power tools in their hands seemed like a potentially dangerous situation. One of the concerns I had as the work weekend got closer was that someone might be injured. Since we would be in a foreign country without knowing its proficiency in responding to an emergency, having a physician on site seemed prudent.

One of my neighbors on Mercer Island, and a fellow parishioner, was a doctor. His practice was in anesthesiology, but I thought his training would be sufficient to address a wound inflicted at a construction site. I called him to arrange a quick meeting, and he invited me over to his house. Once there, I reminded him that the work on our orphanage renovation project was scheduled to start in about four weeks and then explained my safety concern. I told him that I was aware that his training was in a different area of medicine, but I thought he was qualified to handle the kinds of injuries that might occur and that the most important part would be the quick response.

He listened politely and then said, "I have no training in this and would not be comfortable with that responsibility."

Adhering to my commitment to only ask once, I thanked him for his time and hoped he would enjoy the rest of his day.

The next morning, I called Scott Murfey and asked him if he knew of a doctor in the San Diego area who might be willing to volunteer to be at the jobsite for a couple of days. He said that no one came to mind, but he'd check with the guys on the management team and get back to me. Later that afternoon, he called to say that he was given the name of a doctor who owned three medical clinics in Tijuana. Scott didn't know if he'd be interested in sending over one of his doctors, but he thought it would be worth a phone call to make the request. The owner of three medical clinics in Tijuana seemed like a reasonable person to ask for a volunteer, so I agreed to make the call.

The owner of the clinics took my call right away and, fortunately, was fluent in English since my Spanish was limited to about eight words! After I explained the project to him and my safety concern, I asked if he could send over one doctor for two days while the work was underway.

"This sounds like a very admirable undertaking, and I'd like to help," he said. "But, instead of sending a doctor, I think it would be better if I was the one at the orphanage that weekend. Maybe you could give me a paintbrush or a broom to help with the renovation, and if someone gets hurt, I'll call one of my clinics. I can promise you this: if I call and request that a doctor be sent over, they will come right away."

"Thank you very much," I replied. "That sounds perfect, and we'll have a paintbrush waiting for you when you arrive!"

This seemed like a successful recruitment. I had asked for one doctor for two days, and even though I was not going to have a doctor on-site, having someone who could make a qualified doctor respond quickly should be almost as good. What I could never have anticipated was how this was going to evolve.

The clinic owner was present during the workdays, and while we didn't spend any time together, I did note a few times that he was carrying a paintbrush. What I found out later was that our charitable effort to help these orphans touched his heart. At the end of the second day, when the orphans returned, the clinic owner met with Rosa and said that whenever any of the children needed medical attention, she could bring them to one of his clinics on a Sunday, and they would treat them at no charge for the next two years. Rosa told me about his offer later that evening. I was very impressed and called the clinic owner a couple of months later to see if he was still able to make his generous offer.

He said, "I decided to modify the commitment. The way it works now is they can bring the children to any of my clinics on any day of the week, and we will take care of them for free for the next two years."

About three months after that, I was asked to give a presentation on the orphanage renovation, and I wanted to mention the free medical care as one of the unexpected gifts that came as a result of our project. I called the clinic owner to confirm that the clinics were still looking after the children, and he said, "We are still looking after the kids, but I changed the arrangement again."

His comment about changing the commitment had me concerned, so I asked, "What changed?"

"The way it works now is they don't have to come to the clinic. All they have to do is call, and we will send a doctor to the orphanage 24 hours a day, 7 days a week. Also, the free medical treatment will last for as long as I own the clinics and not end after two years."

It just kept happening. My simple request for one doctor for two days turned into free healthcare for all the orphans, with doctors available 24 hours a day to go to the orphanage in perpetuity. This was yet another example of someone bringing their own vision to our project and making it much bigger. Everyone was contributing in a way that matched their skills, so for them it might have seemed like a logical expansion of what they were initially asked to do. From my perspective, watching all these talented people take the project to a new level was a bit overwhelming. My conclusion at the time was that helping those orphans was something that God wanted us to do, and He was nudging them to take action and follow their hearts.

Chapter 14

Meanwhile...The W San Diego

When you open a new hotel, it helps to get the press to write or broadcast positive stories about the property. Readers and listeners tend to ignore paid advertisements. This results in you having to pay for multiple ads to get your message heard. This is not only expensive, it's also not as effective as a well-written article or TV news story in building positive awareness of the new hotel.

W Hotel was a relatively new brand at the time and had done a good job in positioning itself as one of the better lifestyle hotel brands. When the W San Diego opened, there were seventeen

When the W San Diego opened, there were seventeen W hotels, of which I had overseen the development of three, with our pension funds being the majority owner of those three properties. While I had an active role in the design and construction of those properties, my involvement in marketing and operations was more passive.

Before you buy furniture for two or three hundred hotel rooms, you build what the industry refers to as a model room so you can confirm that it looks as good in real life as you thought it would when looking at the interior designer's photographs and hand-drawn pictures.

One of W Hotel's marketing ideas was to build what appeared to be a bedroom by placing a queen-size bed on a trailer behind a truck. Then they surrounded it with a glass enclosure and had two people (models) get into the bed underneath the covers. About two weeks before the hotel's opening, they had the truck pull the "model room" around the city of San Diego in the middle of rush hour, thereby causing a traffic jam and attracting the attention of the local media.

One of the local TV news channels sent a photographer and reporter to film the model room as it worked its way around the city and see if they could get an interview with the models lying in the bed. Their efforts met with some success, and the local station contacted its New York City affiliate and asked if they thought it was entertaining enough for national exposure. The New York affiliate said that if the reporter could get inside the glass enclosure to conduct his interview, it would put it on the national newscast. Within about ten minutes, the reporter convinced the models to let him in, and they immediately went live nationally with the interview.

The reporter asked them why they were riding around in a glass-enclosed bed on the back of a truck, and they quickly explained that it was a model room for the new W San Diego hotel. It was all very impressive. The models were not only good-looking, they were also articulate, as if someone had provided them with a script. This was a clear reminder of why I intentionally left the marketing to the senior W Hotel executives without offering ideas or approvals. If they had asked me ahead of time if it was acceptable to intentionally create a traffic jam during rush hour by putting a couple of models in a bed in a glass enclosure on the back of a truck, I might have told them they were crazy.

One of the design parameters for a lifestyle hotel is to "Look like where you are." As an extreme example, building a hotel that fits in perfectly with Times Square in New York City is not the right design for a hotel on the beach in Hawaii. You have to identify unique architectural aspects of the community, geological conditions, or plant life that define the area. In doing this initial research on San Diego, I was unable to isolate anything in the prevailing architecture, the terrain, or the plant life that we could use to make the hotel look and feel like where it was.

While thinking about the W San Diego's design orientation, I was also working with Steve Wynn in Las Vegas on his proposed Wynn Casino to be located on the Las Vegas Strip. I had agreed to have one of our equity funds be a major partner in the project and was working with Steve on the design of the property. For several months, I spent two days a week in Las Vegas with Steve and his architect, going through overall design and building layout options. Steve is a very creative person. What made it even more interesting was the fact that he had macular degeneration in both eyes, which rendered him blind if what he was looking at moved. To compensate, his architect's drawings were enlarged, and we would study them for a while on the tabletop before sitting down and discussing what we reviewed. One of the consequences of his macular degeneration was the development of perfect recall. He could see every detail in his mind and make mental adjustments based on our discussion.

At one point I asked him what his overall design inspiration was for the property, given that so many of the more successful casinos on the Strip copied famous architecture from around the world. "I decided to follow the best designer on earth" he said. "And that would be God. I studied mountains, lakes, rivers, desert landscapes and starry nights. From that, I found inspiration for how the casino should look, and feel, from the point of arrival to the look of the building and the feeling of the interior elements."

He provided a few examples based on the design progress that far, which I found to be very impressive. On my flight back to Seattle later that day I considered Steve's design inspiration for the Wynn Casino in context of my puzzle over the design of the W San Diego. I wasn't sure what the solution would be, but I liked the 'go with God' direction.

Unfortunately, one of the investors in our equity fund came under investigation by the Department of Labor for having invested too much of its pension fund in a single asset, which was a hotel in Florida. Even though it was a small investor in our equity fund, my partners concluded that it would be inappropriate to have our fund invest in a high-profile hotel in Las Vegas while a federal investigation was underway on one of our fund's participants. One of the most difficult business conversations I've ever had was having to tell Steve Wynn that we could not be his partner in the Casino. To his credit, he said he understood and would miss having me on the team. Then he said, "Goodbye." And that was the last time we ever spoke.

My daughter Blaire is creative and even though she was only sixteen years old at the time, I asked her what she thought were God inspired design aspects of San

Diego I could use to guide our architect and interior designer.

"There are a couple of things that I identify as being God inspired in that part of Southern California", she said.

"And they are?"

"A white sandy beach, a bright blue sky, and dark blue water. I don't know if that will help you with the hotel's design, but it's what comes to mind when I think of San Diego."

"It might help. I have a very creative architect and interior designer, so maybe I should tell them that we want to celebrate the sky, the ocean, and our white sandy beaches and see if that gets their creative juices flowing. Based on past experience with these designers, it won't take too long to find out."

I met with the design team shortly after hearing Blaire's insights and described the inspirations in general terms, without offering any examples of how any of them could be used in the design. As with all my instructions to creative people, I limit my detailed comments to items such as the number of square feet we are allowed to build, the maximum height, our construction and furnishing budget, the profile of the customers we want to attract, and how we want them to feel during their stay. When we discuss the possible design solutions, I never mention colors or shapes, and

I do not show them pictures of another project that I find interesting. When I stick to this formula, the designs they come back with are always closer to the Mona Lisa than the stickman figure I had in my mind.

The design they presented was an excellent celebration of the sky, ocean, and beach, and I was confident that the hotel would be well-received when we opened. As is frequently the case, seeing the building in three dimensions stimulated my imagination in ways that a two-dimensional drawing cannot.

On part of the site was a steam plant that first opened in 1889. It was about thirty feet in height, and the plan was to turn the ground floor into a restaurant and bar and the second floor into meeting space. The hotel tower was built next to the old steam plant, with the two buildings connected on the ground floor. What was not clear from the architectural drawings was that the exterior wall of the steam plant would be exposed on the upper level of the new hotel lobby, resulting in a large flat surface with no articulation. While standing in the lobby of the hotel, when the construction was about 80 percent complete, that blank space didn't feel like it was going to fit in. The goal at that point was to find a way to turn a negative interior design feature into something positive.

Contrary to my usual approach of having the interior designer or architect develop some options, I decided to come up with the solution on my own this time. My starting point was to consider the hotel's design inspiration and see if any ideas came to mind. While looking at the upper-level blank wall and thinking about blue skies, sandy beaches, and dark blue water, it seemed like the best way forward was going to be sky-related. Just painting a sky up there didn't seem like it was going to be enough. Maybe instead of trying to just make it fit in, we could make it a focal point. One way to do that would be to have a very large screen, or a lot of smaller ones, showing a video of the sky at different times of the day that matched what was happening outside. This seemed like a good idea, so I contacted a technology design firm whose founder used to work for Walt Disney Imagineering. He lived in the Seattle area, and his children were friends with mine, so we knew each other socially.

He agreed to take on the assignment and said he would have some ideas for me to review in a couple of weeks. When I went to his studio to see his presentation, he said that he had found a way to create a nine-foot wide by eighteen-foot tall screen to show the sky at different times of the day. He said he could create a video to show the sun coming up in the early morning and then have nice clouds slowly moving across the sky during the day. In the early evening, he would have the sun go down with a beautiful sunset, and at about 9 p.m. have the moon rise, with the moon having the outline of a woman's face with her eyes closed. Then, at about 10:30 p.m., he would have the eyes on the moon's face slowly open and look down toward the lobby bar seating and make a little smile. At about 10:45 p.m., he said her eyes would close again and there would be no more expressions. Finally, about thirty minutes before the lobby bar closed, he would have the moon fade and stars in the shape of constellations appear. It would stay that way until sunrise the next morning.

He said that smaller screens were clearer than the very large ones, and they were also more affordable. Based on this, he said we should have eighteen screens installed where the edges touch. He would write the video program so that each screen would display its own unique part of the larger picture. This way, the people watching the video would perceive it as being on one large screen.

I thought it all sounded brilliant and gave him the approval to go ahead. As anticipated, this became a signature item at the hotel. With everything happening in slow motion, it didn't command the guests' attention. They could watch it for a few moments, or longer if they wished, without getting bored. The changes at different times of the day created some extra interest, especially when the moon would open its eyes and smile at the people below. It took a while for it to be generally known that this happened and when. But once the regular customers figured it out, they tended to stay a little longer to watch it and invited their friends to join them.

The other design change that was pursued after construction started was adding a second bar on the roof of the old steam plant. This one was more expensive to build than the sky video, but it was easier to calculate the revenue increase. The inspiration came during a job walk that took us to the steam plant roof to consider waterproofing options. Once there, I took note of the size of the space and the views. The size was ideal for a stand-alone bar, but the roof was only thirty feet above the street, so the views were mainly of traffic and sidewalks. I couldn't see the ocean or a beach from there, but the top half of the tall surrounding office buildings was interesting, especially with the bright blue sky in the background.

I asked the architect to stand next to me near the edge of the roof and said, "If we built a four-foot wall around the roof, starting about six feet in from the edge, I think that people standing inside the four-foot wall would not be able to see anything at street level. Right?"

The architect, Kurt Jensen, said, "Let me step it off." Then he came in about six feet from the edge of the building, looked around, and said, "I think you should build the wall ten feet in from the edge of the building. That way you can't see any traffic or people walking by anywhere in the downtown area."

That would make the upper parts of the surrounding buildings and the sky all that was visible to the roof bar customers. No parts of the blue ocean were visible from there, but if we covered the area where the customers were standing or sitting with about one foot of sand, then we would have a sandbar. Roof bars were popular at many hotels around the country, but I don't think any of them could be characterized as sandbars, which would make this one unique. I explained this to Kurt, and he agreed that it could become a great destination.

There were going to be some structural improvements required because the roof of the old steam plant was not designed to have 80–100 people standing on it with a foot of sand, but the revenue potential of a popular nightclub justified the extra cost. San Diego's weather was moderate in temperature, and the annual rainfall was low, so we should be able to have it open for most of the year. Later that afternoon, I did a Google search on the temperatures and rainfall by day for the previous eighty years to see how many days per year on average that the sandbar would not be comfortable. As an interesting sidenote, what the daily temperatures revealed from 1920 to 2002 is that, at least in San Diego, the average temperature was going down, not up. What the data also showed was that there was no rain on about 90 percent of the days. During the peak winter months, however, the temperature was frequently lower than desired for an outdoor venue. I considered adding heat lamps to warm up the seating area on those days, but then it occurred to me that a more efficient way to evenly increase the temperature would be to heat the sand with hot water running through pipes about 6–8 inches below the surface.

I asked Kurt if he thought this was a good idea, and he said, "Wow, that's brilliant. I'll draw it that way."

One of the lessons I learned while working in private equity, where we had about two billion dollars to invest every year in real estate projects, was that when talking with architects, construction companies, developers, and lenders, my ideas that used to be considered 'fine' were now characterized as 'brilliant.' My attempts at humor that used to get a chuckle occasionally now resulted in hysterical laughter, and no one ever interrupted me when I was talking. I was grateful that I didn't get this job before I was in my mid-forties, so I was able to not internalize this glowing feedback. Unfortunately, most of the people I interacted with who entered the private equity community in their mid to late twenties fell prey to this flattering social mirror and came to believe that they were always the smartest person in the room and were gifted in every subject that came up.

I decided to take my son, Nick, and daughter, Blaire, to Kurt's design review session. Nick, at age 22, was working as a waiter at a popular Seattle restaurant while taking a break from his college degree program at Ohio State University. Blaire was still in high school, but her creative advice had already added value to the design, so I wanted to see if she had any more insights. They also had both shown interest in hotel designs when I brought home construction drawings, spread them out on the dining room table, and explained some of the fun aspects. This, however, was the first time I took them to the architect's office while the designs were still in process.

Kurt's preliminary layout of the sandbar included one bar, wood decking on two of the four sides of the "beach" area, and the proposed location of four cabanas. Kurt and I talked through some of the operational logistics, which seemed to have been properly considered: seating capacity, views, and how warm we could get the sand when the water running through the pipes was at its maximum temperature. When we had gotten most of the way through these design review topics, I asked Nick if he had any thoughts.

He said, "If the seating capacity at the sandbar is 120 people, you will need more than the two pour-stations at the bar. I think you should have a second bar with two more pour stations and put it here." He then pointed to a spot that was near the small service elevator and about forty feet from the one Kurt had drawn.

"That looks like a really good idea," I said. "How many pour stations do you think we'll need behind the new bar?"

"One should do it for 120 people, but on a busy night I think more than 120 people will squeeze into that bar. That means more drinks to pour and more congestion, so I think you should have two pour stations behind both bars."

I glanced over at Kurt to see his reaction, and he shrugged his shoulders and said, "No problem."

I said, "Okay, let's do it. Blaire, do you have any ideas?"

"The wood boards, where they touch the sand, all have a straight edge," Blaire said. "But if you think about the shape of the sand on a beach at the edge of the water, it goes back and forth, like a wave. I think it would look more natural if the deck curved where it touched the sand." As she explained the concept, she moved her finger in the shape of an S to help us visualize the contour she was recommending.

I turned to Kurt and said, "Do it."

Good design is the sum total of hundreds of decisions. There is rarely only one feature that dominates the design in a successful lifestyle hotel. Pictures of furniture on a design board or in a catalog do not tell you whether it's comfortable to sit in. I always have a sample of every chair being considered delivered to the jobsite and then have someone sit in it for three to four hours and report back on whether it was comfortable and for how long. Furniture comfort also changes based on the age of the customer. A 22-year-old can sit on a stool for two hours and think it's comfortable the whole time, whereas a 55-year-old sitting on that same stool would be ready to leave after about twenty minutes.

Ergonomics is important, making the selection of all furniture a combination of both art and science. If you find a nice-looking and comfortable chair for your restaurant and you buy 100 of them, they would probably look okay. But putting 100 identical chairs in your lobby, bar, or nightclub is a mistake because it makes the room look ordinary. The goal should be to create multiple seating arrangements that appear to be in the 'same family' but are not 'twins.'

The music being played affects the perception of visual elements and can affect the energy in the room. As with the furniture, music is both an art and a science. Plus, it's important to change the music based on the time of day and the day of the week. There needs to be a beat because that gives the room energy, and you need to avoid popular songs about how someone broke their heart in a romantic relationship because the listener oftentimes associates it with a sad time in their life.

The volume is also important. Ideally, the music should be 5 decibels above ambient noise in the room. We accomplish this by installing the speakers twelve feet apart so everyone in the room hears the music at the same volume, and then we install sound attenuators that read the decibel level during a two-second gap between songs and adjust the music volume accordingly. If done properly, the music is a welcome third voice in the conversation no matter where you're standing or sitting and no matter how many people are in the room.

All the lighting in the public areas has a mild yellow tint, so it makes the skin of the people in the room appear to have a nice tan, regardless of the natural color of their skin.

Artwork is an aspect of interior design, but preferences change over time, with a popular painting potentially going out of style in a year or two. One way to keep it current is to offer local artists the ability to display their paintings on the walls of your hotel's public areas. We always have some art pieces that are permanent, and many are provided by our artists in residence—local artists whose paintings we feature for about six months. This not only keeps the overall design fresh, it also creates interest in the hotel from the artist's followers and gives the local media a new story to write about.

The combination of getting recognized by the local and national media, having a sandbar on the roof, visual technology in our lobby created by a former designer from Walt Disney Imagineering, comfortable seating, great music, curated lighting, and an overall design that resonated with southern California resulted in the hotel being full with lines out the door and around the block from the first day we opened. The San Diego hotel market report from Smith Travel Research showed that, within a couple of months of opening, the W San Diego had the highest room revenue per available room (RevPAR) in the downtown San Diego area, and the owner of the W brand, Starwood Lodging, hosted its annual stockholders meeting at the hotel in January 2003 to highlight the quality of new hotels it was adding to its portfolio.

At the grand opening of the hotel in January 2003, I brought my son Nick and my daughter Blaire to the event. It was a great party and well attended. About halfway through the evening, I took them to the sandbar to show them how it looked in real life. The crowd was fully engaged and seemed to be enjoying the experience.

After walking around the sand and deck, checking out the space from different perspectives, I pointed to the curved wooden deck and said, "Blaire, a year ago that was just an idea in your mind and now it is the centerpiece of the most popular nightclub in San Diego. Thank you, and enjoy the moment."

I then turned to Nick, who was over 21 years old at the time, and asked, "Can I get you a drink from the bar you created?"

He smiled and said, "With pleasure."

The following year, Blaire entered architectural school at the University of Southern California, and ten years later she was designing bars and restaurants at popular destinations in Los Angeles and Las Vegas. Nick decided to leave the world of food and beverage operations and now is a product manager for a division of Microsoft where they create platforms for video games.

Chapter 15

More Volunteers Than We Needed

Two weeks before the Tijuana orphanage's renovation was scheduled, the W Hotel was nearly completed, and it was deemed safe to directly recruit some construction workers. Ken Summers recommended that I be the one to make the request and that it be done during the workers' lunch break in the hotel restaurant's dining area. I thought it would be good to have the manager of the orphanage present, so I invited Rosa to join me and say a few things about the children and the need for the repairs. The presentation was going to start around noon, but Rosa arrived at about 9 a.m. because she took public transportation. So we had some extra time to prepare. I invited her to a late breakfast at a nearby restaurant where we could talk about the presentation.

I thought it might be helpful for me to know the background on how the children came to Casa Hogar de Los Ninos. I assumed that they were assigned to the orphanage by a Mexican governmental agency or maybe a local charitable organization. We haven't had orphanages in the US for a long time, so I was not familiar with the process.

Once we were settled in at the breakfast table, I asked, "Rosa, tell me how the children end up at the orphanage."

"One of the boys, Richy, who is now eight years old, was dropped off by his parents. They said they were doing some work on their house about a mile away and needed a place for him to stay for about two weeks. We took him in, thinking it was going to be temporary. After about three weeks, his parents had not yet returned, and one night Richy disappeared. I got a call from the night manager, who said Richy was missing, so I drove to the neighborhood where his parents said they lived. I figured he would be close to there, looking for his mom and dad. I found him sitting on the sidewalk, crying. He was lost and couldn't find his family's home. I took him back to the orphanage, and the next day I looked up his parents' address and went there to check on the status of the repair work they told me about. What I found was an empty house. I asked one of the neighbors where the owners could be found, and they said that they moved out three weeks ago and didn't tell anyone where they were going.

"Richy has been with us for two years now. He was very sad for quite a while, but lately he has started to make some friends."

That was not what I expected her to say. Having your parents die or give you up at birth is sad, but to be abandoned by your family because they don't want you is far worse. I said, "How many of the children are just left at your front gate while the parents drive away?"

"They come to us for many reasons. We take them in if the family died or just doesn't want them anymore. Either way, they are orphans and have nowhere else to go."

It was heartbreaking to hear this, but instead of making me sad or angry, it filled my veins with adrenaline. The people running this orphanage were doing God's work, and they needed our help. My commitment was to not convince workers to volunteer using salesmanship, but I suspected that this next presentation was going to be a little different.

When the workers had assembled in the hotel's restaurant for their lunch break, I introduced Rosa as the manager of the Casa Hogar de Los Ninos orphanage, who had an important message for them. Rosa was great with children and managing an orphanage, but public speaking was not one of her strengths. After a couple of minutes describing the orphanage and the care they provide for children, she said, "Thank you." And sat down.

At that point, I stepped forward to address the approximately 100 workers in the room. "I want to give you a brief description of one of the orphans that Rosa cares for. He was abandoned by his parents when he was six years old. They told Rosa that he would only be at the orphanage for a couple of weeks, but they never came back for him. It has now been two years. I don't know how to minister to a child like that, and neither do you. We are not counselors, doctors, or church workers, but we can fix that orphan's home. They don't have enough working bathrooms, the electrical wiring is faulty, they have no heat, and people come into the orphanage at night and steal what few possessions these children have. This is something that we can fix. We have the work planned out, and the materials will be on-site. What we need are skilled tradesmen who can help us fix this broken building—in two days.

"I will be there, and so will the Webcor team, including Ross Edwards Sr. and Jr. In two days, you can change the lives of all fifty-five orphans, including the one who was abandoned by his parents. Work starts at 6:30 a.m. on Saturday, December 14, and ends thirty-six hours later. We'll provide the meals and a place to stay on Friday and Saturday night if you don't want to do the commute. In January your friends are going to ask, 'What did you give the kids for Christmas this year?' I think you're going to want to tell them that you gave them a 'new life.' I will be here for the rest of the afternoon. If this is something you can help us with, please come by and let me know or let the Webcor team know today or later. Thank you, and I hope to see you in Tijuana."

About twenty-five workers came by my table that afternoon to let me know they would be coming to Tijuana for the workdays. Two days later, we received a message from the local plumbers' union that they had another fifty plumbers willing to come to the orphanage that weekend. After checking with Ken, we decided that we had enough plumbers on the volunteer list already and gratefully declined to have the additional workers. I didn't think we'd ever be in a situation where we had more volunteers than we needed. I wasn't sure we'd be in that situation for all the construction trades, but the number of volunteers in all disciplines was getting close to the target.

The children needed to be away from the orphanage on the workdays. Mercer Island Presbyterian Church had recruited twenty-five high school students to work with the orphanage employees to help the children pack up and move to a small Tijuana motel about twenty miles from the orphanage for the weekend. I thought it might be awkward to have a couple of hundred workers staring at the children when they returned on Sunday evening, after the work was completed. I knew it would be important for the workers to see the children's reaction to their new home, so I thought the best way to accomplish this would be to film the renovation work and then the children's return and have a video of this delivered to all the workers before Christmas Day. My initial assumption was that we could have Blaire do the filming, but as always, a better option didn't take long to present itself. Someone in Hollywood heard about the renovation, and I received a call from a professional documentary filmmaker. He wanted to be paid something modest but agreed to have the final version completed by Christmas Day so the workers would all have a copy of the documentary film. I think Blaire would have made a great movie, but with Hollywood being the other option, she was reassigned to look after the orphans on the work weekend.

The closer we got to the work weekend, the more stressful it seemed. Opening a high-profile hotel in a major market is enough to cause anxiety all by itself. Having the same people plan and then execute a large compressed-build project at the same time could be too much. Fortunately, of the 300 people playing an active role in the execution of the orphanage renovation, only about eight had senior executive roles in the hotel project. For them, the last two to three weeks before the workdays were composed of long days and restless nights.

The night before the first workday, I hosted a dinner at the Sheraton San Diego – Harbor Island. The hotel's general manager, Joe Tersi, had not only agreed to donate some of the food to the orphanage, but he had also volunteered to be one of the cooks at the orphanage on the workdays. This seemed odd to me because he'd be working alongside the president of the local hotel union. It's not normal for the general manager of a 1,000-room hotel to spend personal time with the person who convinced his employees to join the union. The wisdom he demonstrated in doing this is probably one of the reasons Joe later became the president of the San Diego Convention and Visitor Bureau. The dinner event was well attended, with about 200 of the local and Seattle-based volunteers enjoying the meal and hopefully motivated by my pep talk.

Chapter 16

D-Day

All the volunteers were at the orphanage by 6:30 a.m. on the morning of December 14, 2002. The building materials had been loaded into four semitruck trailers and were on their way to the US and Mexican border. Their expected arrival time was 7 a.m., which would allow us to start the process shortly thereafter. At about 6:45 a.m., I received a call from one of the truck drivers. He was at the border and the Mexican guard did not accept their explanation for the use of all the building materials. The drivers had explained that it was for the renovation of Casa Hogar de Los Ninos, a charitable project undertaken to make the orphanage a safer place for the children, but the guard believed that the drivers' intent was to sell the materials and they were trying to avoid paying the tariff.

I asked the driver, "How much does he want you to pay?"

"Four thousand seven hundred dollars."

This sounded like blackmail, with the border guard intending to pocket the money. I told the driver, "Stand by, and I'll call you right back."

Ross Edwards and his father were standing near me when I received the call, and they asked me if there was a problem. I explained what the driver told me and said that this was not fair, and we should not have to pay a bribe to that border guard to get those materials. I told them that I was going to get the filmmaker to come with me to the border and get this on film so we could hold the Mexican government accountable.

Ross Edwards Sr. asked me to calm down and let him take care of this problem. I agreed with him that my anger was probably not going to be helpful in resolving the situation and said that him taking over was probably a good idea. I was not sure how Ross Sr. was going to fix the situation, but he and his son left promptly in their car and headed toward the border.

About twenty-five minutes later, Ross Jr. and Sr. returned, followed by four semitrucks full of materials. I didn't ask them how they resolved the problem, assuming that they'd tell me later if they thought I'd agree with their method. It's been twenty-two years since the work weekend, and the subject has never come up, but I

98

do agree that whatever they did resulted in a successful outcome.

On the job site, we thought it would be helpful to be able to readily identify the professional builders versus the unskilled volunteers. To make this easy, we ordered two types of T-shirts; one was blue and had the word "Varsity" written on the back, and the other one was yellow, and it had "Junior Varsity" written on the back. The professional builders were the varsity, and the rest were junior varsity. To most people's surprise, I wore a junior varsity T-shirt on the workdays because I had very little experience with tools and, over the years, I came to understand that my aptitude in construction-related work was below average. Given that the last four generations of men in my family were either carpenters, wood-carvers, or cabinetmakers, and that I had completed more than 100 hotel transactions that involved either new construction or a heavy renovation, my having poor construction skills seems, for most people, to be counterintuitive. When I told the leadership team that I would be wearing the junior varsity T-shirt, they smiled a little, a puzzled expression on their faces, but they did not challenge my decision.

While we were waiting for the materials to arrive, the workers were touring the facilities to assess the layout and conceptualize the logistics. They also started some of the demolition and relocated furniture items that would be in the way of the intended work areas.

Once the materials arrived and the repairs and construction commenced, I studied the movement of the workers around the property and their focus of attention. For about the first ninety minutes, it looked a little chaotic with so many workers in a comparatively small area. After the first ninety minutes, however, it started looking like a ballet. Everyone got oriented to the workspace and was focused on their part of the project.

In a normal construction project, the workers take turns working in a particular area. As an example, if you are building a wall inside a building, the first tradesmen that go in are the carpenters, who install structural wood. Based on the size of the job, this can take anywhere from several days to several months. When they have completed this first step, the electricians go into that area and install the wiring for the plugs and lighting fixtures.

As with the carpenters, the time it takes to do this work depends on the size of the project and the number of electricians assigned to the job. Next go the plumbers. Then the drywall installers go in and nail in the walls, followed by the painters. Then the finish carpenters go in and put in the wood trim. The electricians go back and install the lighting fixtures and cover plates on electrical plugs, followed by the plumbers, who install the bathroom fixtures. The last ones in install the fixtures, like mirrors, countertops, signage, pictures, doors, and carpeting.

The time it takes to do all this is affected by:

- the number of people assigned to each task
- the availability of the needed materials
- the predictability of the competition time of the tradesmen assigned to do the part prior to the next tradesmen being given access to the building

For example, if ten drywallers arrive when scheduled to begin their part of the project but the carpenters had not completed their part due to either too few carpenters assigned or a shortage of needed materials, that can create unnecessary delays. And it can potentially result in some of the other trades reassigning their workers to another project.

In a compressed-build approach, with several hundred workers at the jobsite, each of these tasks is completed within an hour or two, with each trade going into that part of the building within a few minutes after the last trade's completion. With the unskilled volunteers carrying the materials, doing the cleanup, and assisting with all the tasks that do not require technical training, the skilled tradesmen can spend more time doing the parts that they alone are qualified to do.

I spent most of my time over the two workdays walking around the buildings to see if we had enough volunteers working on a particular aspect to get it done quickly. If the lead tradesman in that area said he needed more workers, I would go and find ones that were over-assigned in another area and get them relocated. When I wasn't moving the workers around the building, I went to the kitchen, got a large bowl of chocolate cookies, and delivered them to the workers. As noted earlier, on the workdays, I was junior varsity.

By the middle of the afternoon on Saturday, we had made significant progress on most of our repair items. No one needed to go to the local lumberyard or tool shop to buy anything we'd overlooked or forgotten. The volunteers all seemed to be in good spirits because of the progress they were making. It was interesting to see how our junior varsity workers were demonstrating that they had an aptitude for some of the skilled trades. It had not occurred to me that a lawyer or physician could work alongside a carpenter and make a meaningful contribution to the construction effort. They were not just fetching materials. With a little instruction, they were able to assemble or repair parts of the building. In a different life, I could see how, with proper instruction and enough time on jobsites, this could have been their occupation.

Having spent several of my formative years on my father's job sites, working alongside skilled tradesmen, I was able to recognize the aptitude in others and the absence thereof in me. Fortunately, envisioning what needed to be done and organizing the effort did match my skillset, but once on an active construction jobsite, my most useful contribution was fetching cookies for the workers.

The sunlight began to fade in the early evening, so most of the workers packed up their tools at about 5 p.m. and made their way to the kitchen to take part in the evening meal. The food was good, with most of the conversations being a discussion about what needed to happen next to finish by the end of the day on Sunday. The orphanage's bedrooms needed to be finished by noon because that's when the volunteers, whose assignment was to get them ready for the children's return, would arrive with the cleaning equipment and the personalized pillows. We weren't sure of the exact time when the children and management team would return, but I wanted most, if not all, the workers to have left by then. We didn't need them there when the children returned to the completed renovation and expansion of their home. The workers would receive their copy of the documentary film before Christmas Day, which would hopefully have captured the children's expressions of joy and gratitude.

Some of the workers who lived close to the US and Mexican border went home on Saturday night, but most had brought a sleeping bag and sought out a clean room within the orphanage complex to spend the night. I was feeling the stress of needing to complete everything by the early evening on Sunday and started walking around the complex looking for areas that needed extra attention. Some of the workers were, apparently, also feeling this stress and continued working on their part of the project for a few hours after dinner.

My most vivid memory of that evening, as I walked through every room in the orphanage, was hearing gunfire in the neighborhood. I knew that Tijuana was rated as the most dangerous city in the world, so I shouldn't have been surprised, but it caused me to feel tension and was a clear reminder of why we were building the security fence around the compound.

At about 11 p.m. that night, I found an open spot on the floor for my sleeping bag. I don't know why it hadn't occurred to me that I should bring a pillow, probably because I had other things on my mind. So, I didn't have a restful sleep that night due to the hard floor and having to use my arm for a pillow.

Everyone was up early the next morning, and after breakfast, they were ready to finish the job. I started my walk around the complex, looking for projects that needed more labor. I noted that only two of the four welders were working on the security fence. One of the welders was the artist who volunteered after hearing about the project in my meeting with the union official.

I asked him, "Where are the other two guys who were here yesterday?"

"They decided to go to a bar in Tijuana last night and apparently drank too much. They called me this morning and said they were too hungover to be here today."

"You have got to be kidding me. We only have four welders. Do you think you two can finish it today?"

"We'll try, but getting all around the property by this evening is going to be a challenge."

Then I walked to where a large dump truck was parked. Steve Bremner, the chief financial officer of Kennedy Associates and my co-worker, had taken on the assignment of cleaning up the jobsite. This included the trash that we created as well as the waste materials that were there when we arrived. He had been very busy but had not asked for any help.

I asked him, "So, Steve, how many times have you filled up that dump truck?"

"I filled it up three times yesterday and took it to the dump site. My best guess is there's another two loads remaining."

"Five dump trucks full of garbage! That's about four more than I thought you were going to say. Let me know if you need any help, and I'll send over some extra manpower."

"Thanks, but I own this one and will have it done by the end of the day."

The septic tank was about thirty feet from where the dump truck was parked. The tanks are placed in what is referred to as a leach field, which is about an acre of vacant land behind the orphanage. Three of the plumbers were working on the pipes that connected the septic tank to the orphanage.

I asked them, "You got it figured out?"

"There were two problems," one of the plumbers said. "The drainage pipe was clogged with debris, and not the good kind. We got that cleaned out. The other issue is the septic tank is full, and we don't have the right equipment here to deal with that."

"Do you know where we can find what you need?" I asked.

"This is going to take specialized equipment, a truck, and people who do this kind of thing every day. We called one of our subs, and he agreed to do it, but he can't get here today. Tomorrow is the soonest."

"Tomorrow?" I asked.

"Yeah, tomorrow. But he's a good guy, and we trust that he'll do what he said."

"Thanks. Is everything else working okay?" I asked.

"I think we got the rest of it fixed. The only other thing left to do is tie in the new bathroom on the second floor," he said.

I gave him a thumbs-up and decided to go to the second floor and check on the status of the new bathroom. Once there, I saw that there was only one worker in the new bathroom, and he was focused on getting the walls trimmed out and painted. I recognized him right away, since he was my son Nick! Nick did not have any construction experience but was fortunate to have inherited the craftsman genes from his ancestors. The high aptitude, coupled with some good instruction from the Webcor team, allowed him to create the bathroom enclosure in one weekend.

He watched as I surveyed the room from top to bottom and seemed to be expecting negative feedback. This was his first construction assignment that had to be completed at a fast pace, and he was not paired with an experienced carpenter, so his expression of mild anxiety while waiting for my comment was not surprising.

"Did the plumbers say when this needs to be finished?" I asked.

"The pipes are already installed," Nick said. "The only thing left is setting the toilet in place and connecting the sink when the counter is installed. They said it wouldn't take long once I was done with the walls and door. Based on my progress so far, my guess is that I'll be done by lunch."

I gave him a thumbs-up and continued my tour. Because we had more plumbers than we needed for a two-day completion of that part of the project, they decided to install an irrigation system in the front yard to keep the grass, trees, and flowers healthy. The plumbers had finished the irrigation system's installation by Saturday afternoon, and they were testing it to see if the sprinklers had the right coverage. I think they also did some pruning because the landscaping looked very nice and there were no weeds.

The tile workers had a very effective system in place for getting the floors covered in the boys' section of the dormitory. They had one man on a table saw, one man to measure the size of the tile that abutted the walls, three men laying the tile, one man telling the cutter the size of the tile piece they needed, and one person delivering the cut tile to the work area. At a normal jobsite, they wouldn't segment it like this. They would have maybe one man on the saw, and then the installer would take the measurements, tell the cutter what he needed, wait for the piece or pieces to be trimmed, and then take it back to the floor area they were working on and glue down the tile. Both systems work, but dividing up the tasks between cutters, installers, and runners allows the installation to happen a lot faster. By mid-morning it seemed like they would be finished within a couple of hours.

Just before the lunch break, three people from the W Hotel's housekeeping staff arrived with the pillows that had the children's names sewn onto them, the

Christmas presents, and some cleaning supplies. It was going to require someone from the orphanage staff to make sure the pillows were delivered to the right rooms and tell us where to hide the Christmas presents, but all the bedrooms and most of the other rooms in the compound were ready to be cleaned. The volunteers were all fully engaged, and it looked like the extensive scope of work was going to be completed, with the exception of the security fence and maybe the storage shed for the home-building materials. The senior construction management team from Webcor had taken on the job of building the storage shed. When I asked them if they wanted me to reassign some carpenters to help them, they said they had it under control, so I moved on.

The new food storage room was done, and the six tons of food had been placed on shelves. Ross Edwards Sr. and Jr. had taken on the job of building a new staircase on the outside of the dormitory building. This provided access to several second-floor bedrooms that could accommodate twenty additional orphans. By mid-afternoon on Sunday, the staircase was completed. The mechanical crew finished the installation of a heater at about the same time, which would keep the children warm on those cold winter days.

By 5 p.m. almost all the work had been completed. The workers were packing up their tools, cleaning up the compound, or sitting in a chair giving their sore muscles some relief. This was especially the case with the junior varsity members, who spend most of their regular workdays sitting at a desk or standing in a courtroom and not handling heavy building materials. The mood of the workers seemed to be more one of relief than celebration, which was understandable.

Renovating in two days an entire orphanage that could now accommodate seventy-five children was a major undertaking. Ironically, the more you know about construction, the less possible it seemed that this much work could be done in such a short time. But here we were. Even the storage shed got done, leaving only the security fence. Other than a few sore muscles, there were no injuries.

The children and staff were supposed to start arriving back at the orphanage at 6 p.m. Most of the workers had departed when the cars and buses started to arrive with the children. The filmmaker had chosen a place to stand with his camera, hoping to capture the children's reaction when they began to see the improvements that had been made. He spent several hours that evening conducting interviews with the staff and older children, recording their expressions of gratitude and, at times, tearful responses. As promised, he had the documentary film completed in about a week, and we were able to get a copy to all the workers by Christmas Day. The filmmaker was not, however, able to personalize each copy by having the worker's name in the opening shot. It turned out to be too time-consuming for the filmmaker, working alone, to get 300 different versions of the film completed in one week. Despite that, I think the film was appreciated, not just by the volunteers who did the work but also by their children, who were able to see that at least on those two days their father was a good man.

It took two months for the welders to complete the security fence around the orphanage. A couple of them would drive down from San Diego for a few hours in the evening, several times a week, until the fencing was fully attached and secure.

Some of the volunteers from my church would tease me about this, saying, "The ONE thing you didn't get done that weekend was the whole reason you went down there in the first place." They would say this while smiling, and after the fence was finally completed, I was able to smile back and appreciate the irony.

Chapter 17

Madrona Grace and Gratitude

Expressing gratitude in a way that compares to the kindness that you were shown in a time of need cannot always be done with a few words or even said to the person who provided the gift. My business decisions and world events converged to create a problem that I could not resolve on my own. Receiving financial help from a fellow parishioner during a particularly vulnerable point in time meant a lot to me and my family. Expressing our appreciation with kind words and a handshake did not seem enough.

Finding someone with a problem that they could not solve without my help seemed like the best way to bring personal closure to my need to say, "Thank you." There are many organizations that provide charitable services to people in need whose buildings are broken.

What I learned from renovating Casa Hogar de Los Ninos is that God blesses many of these ministries, and if you help the people who are doing God's work, you get help in ways that cannot always be predicted. Asking for a doctor to volunteer for two days at the jobsite evolved into free healthcare for the orphans in perpetuity. I asked for two cooks for two days and ended up with six tons of food and an offer from the San Diego Food Bank to continue giving the orphanage food supplies whenever they asked.

What started out as a weekend project for me and five or six welders to build a security fence around the orphanage evolved into 300 volunteers renovating the entire compound. All along the way, people were being nudged by the Holy Spirit to expand the project to a much different level. One thing I know for sure is the volunteers were not motivated to join the effort because of my high-energy sales pitch. Their motivation came from within.

One of the consequences of recruiting volunteers from a large audience is that the word gets out that you can do large construction projects in just a few days. A few months after the completion of the orphanage project, someone from my church asked me to inspect the roof of a church in Seattle that had a predominantly African American congregation. It sounded like an easy project for a church that was active in the community, so I agreed to do the inspection.

Spring was not far away, and the weather was getting warmer, and the rainfall was a little less. On the day I first visited Madrona Grace Presbyterian Church to see what might be causing the roof leak, I was greeted by Marla Washington, the senior pastor, and Fordie Ross, one of the church's older parishioners. My expectation was they would show me where to enter the attic space and point to the areas where there was water damage. That did happen during my visit, but they also wanted to explain to me the history of the church so I could better understand their journey and why they were asking for our help.

Fordie started off by saying, "In 1952, the Seattle Presbytery contacted our Session" (which is the name of a Presbyterian church's leadership committee) "and said that they wanted to merge our congregation with the one at Madrona Grace Presbyterian Church, which was located about ten blocks away from our church at the time. They said that they would sell our church and use the proceeds to fix up Madrona Grace. We weren't excited about losing our church, but we wanted to be loyal to the Presbytery, so we agreed. Our last worship service in our old church was on Easter Sunday in 1952. The next Sunday we came here, but apparently the Presbytery didn't tell them we were coming because they looked very surprised when we came into the sanctuary—and not in a good way. The next Sunday, there were half as many white people at the service as the week before, and within a month, all of Madrona Grace's white parishioners had left the church. It made us feel ashamed. The church building was not in very good condition, but we thought there would be enough money from the sale of our old church to pay for the repairs. But then the Presbytery decided not to give us the money. Instead, they bought the land on Mercer Island where Mercer Island Presbyterian Church is now located. It didn't seem right, for a lot of reasons, with the big one being that our congregation paid for our church with our own money and with no help from the Presbytery. Right now, we have $15,000 to get our roof repaired and are hoping that you can find a way to make that possible, since the estimate we got from a roofing company came to about $200,000."

"I might be able to help you with the roof, but before we check it out, I'd like to walk through the entire church," I said.

Neither Fordie nor the pastor said anything. They just stood up and pointed at the conference room door, and led me on the tour. About an hour later, I was feeling the adrenaline and suspected that I had been set up by my church. They asked me to look at the roof, knowing that the condition of the church building and the backstory were going to lead to something more once I heard about their past and saw the current condition of the church.

When I got back home, I called Bill McFarlane, the senior executive at the Seattle Presbytery. I knew Bill and wanted to verify the troubling story I had just been told by Fordie Ross at Madrona Presbyterian Church. I relayed to Bill a summary of the story that Fordie explained to me about how they had lost their church and that the money from the sale of their church was used to buy the land on Mercer Island where my church is now located.

"Everything you said is true, but it gets worse," Bill said. "When the two church congregations were merged back in 1952, the Presbytery had to decide which of the two pastors was going to stay and which one was going to be fired. Even after the white members of Madrona Grace abandoned the church, the Presbytery made the church keep the white pastor and fire the one that the African American congregation had brought with them. That decision, along with several others over the next ten years, made it hard for Madrona Grace to stay on course. But, as testimony to their good hearts, they stayed loyal and have survived for the last fifty years."

I thanked Bill for his honesty and ended the call. At my house, we have a string of bells on the door leading to the backyard that our two dogs have learned to swat when they want to go outside. I watched as they walked together to the door, with Dixey—the older of the two Havanese—slapping the chain. I decided to go outside with them and sat in a chair on the porch. The flowers were beginning to bloom and there was a sweet smell in the air.

I called one of my real estate broker friends who focused on Mercer Island and asked him, "If the Mercer Island Presbyterian Church land was vacant, how much would it sell for today?"

He said, "You could probably build about five houses on it, which would make it worth about $1,000,000."

When the call ended, I started mentally adding up the retail cost to each of the physical problems that I saw earlier in the day during my inspection of Madrona Grace. To do a more detailed estimate would take several weeks, but I already knew in my heart what the total retail cost would be for those repairs. If I were to take on this project, I would have $15,000 to complete about $1,000,000 worth of work. The only way to do that is with volunteer labor and donated materials. I bowed my head in prayer and said, "Lord, is this something you want me to do?" I could feel the chill through my body that comes with a release of adrenaline. Great. I was still stressed out from the last extreme makeover, and now He wants me to do another one!

Five months of planning and three working weekends later, the Madrona Grace Presbyterian Church had a new roof, new windows, a new kitchen and choir loft, remodeled bathrooms and office space, new doors, a new pulpit, and the interior was completely repainted, and a new sound system in the sanctuary.

As it was with the orphanage, we started off with nothing and ended up with everything. I would like to report that after these two extreme makeovers, I was able to spend all my business hours on my hotel projects. But it didn't work that way. By 2010, I had completed eight extreme makeovers, was invited onto the board of directors of three faith-based universities, and in 2017 was presented the Vision from the Mountain Top award by the Seattle-based African American faith community on Martin Luther King Day. There have been numerous other mission trips and presentations, all of which came as the result of an act of kindness from someone to whom a meaningful thank you was not possible. Many of these charitable efforts created stress at the time, but after years of reflection, they were all worth it.

About the Author

Jack is a founding partner of Hartland Hotel Group, which specializes in hotel design, development, and operational consulting. Jack has been involved in over 300 hotel transactions, of which almost one-third involved either new construction or heavy renovation. Several of his hotels have won national and international awards, such as Best New Lifestyle Hotel in the World, Hotel of the Year, Best Hotel Design, and Best Chef in Boston (Liberty Hotel), the Best New Restaurant in Manhattan (W Union Square), and in 2024 the 4th Best Hotel Restaurant and the 3rd Best Hotel Bar in the United States (Hotel Figueroa).

Jack brought his professional training and experience to philanthropic projects, which included the extreme makeover of churches, buildings dedicated to charitable causes, and an orphanage in Tijuana, Mexico. He has also been on the board of directors of four faith-based organizations over the past twenty years. When not working, he enjoys fishing in Canada and playing golf with his grandson.